# How to Market Your Home Staging Business

The Ultimate Guide To Building A Successful

Home Staging Business So That You Can Finally

Turn Your Passion Into Profits

**Fabienne Raphaël, Marketing Expert**

*I dedicate this book to Kristin and my 2 favorite*

*soccer players.*

**Table of Content**

# INTRODUCTION

The Real Estate Market is unstable. Your financial security is also unstable. Sometimes, business is good, and sometimes, it's not. Sometimes, quick money is made - sometimes, it takes months before the money comes in.

How to Market Your Home Staging Business: The Ultimate Guide to Building a Successful Home Staging Business so that You Can Finally Turn Your Passion into Profits, is for you, Home Stagers who are wondering if you have what it takes to be successful, but also to know if you are applying what essential marketing elements you need to apply to your business.

This book has been written to help you to stand above your competitors.

Do You Want To Receive Free Bonuses?  If you do, go to www.marketingtocrushyourcompetitors.com/contact-me/ and start your message with Send Me My Bonuses!

When you do, you will receive:

- A mind map and a document on Home Staging Business Owner Success Plan

- 5 best online tools for Home Staging Business Owners

- A Getting Started With Your Home Staging Business Checklist

# CHAPTER 1

## Do I Have What It Takes To Be A Home Staging Business Owner And Generate Sales?

Let's see. You need a trilogy that is very important. You need media presence, you need public relations, and you need marketing. When we talk about media presence, we have to say that people buy people, and people buy from people they know, people they like, and people they trust. So usually, when someone sees a personality in the media, well, that person is automatically seen as an authority.

All of a sudden, being on television, being heard on the radio, being seen on the internet makes the person even more important, and even be seen as an expert. The more you can share on social media, the better it is for you. You can write a book, you can have your website, you can give interviews, or you can be on the radio. Whatever media presence you can add to your CV or to who you are, the better it is. Remember, as soon as people see you or hear you in the media, you're automatically an expert.

Public relations is all about networking. Of course nowadays, everybody speaks about the internet, how important it is to have a website, how important it is to be on social media, and how important it is to be sitting in front of the computer for a few hours every day in order to communicate with your audience directly through social media, or just to add new things to your blog or to your website, plus keep everything updated. But the thing is, networking is very strong because when people see you in person, they can actually refer to you better.

Most sales are done when the person is facing you, because people see what you look like; they pick up on your charisma, they are aware that your whole personality is working to get that sale, or to maintain this relationship with them. Basically when you network, people see you, so they then have a reference that you actually exist for real. This is good for you.

You also must have marketing. A lot of people forget about that part. They build the website. They do business cards. They are all excited about it, but if you don't tell people you exist, nobody is going to find you. You decide to publish a book, but if there's no marketing into letting people know that your book exists, nobody is going to buy it.

What's important about the marketing though is that you are your business's best marketer, meaning, you know which objective you want to accomplish within the next six months, within the next year. You know how much it means to you to have that business. You know that this business is very important because it supports your family. You know that your business is like your baby and you really want to get it to the next level.

By giving the opportunity to some marketing professional to take care of it, on his own without questioning you about your target market, who you want to target, where you want to market, which way you want to market, and what's the best way for you to market .....
Actually, it means you're not working with the

right person. Sometimes a marketing agency just takes a file and tells you, "Okay, don't worry. I'll take care of it myself and I'll do it for you."

The thing is that those marketing companies are thinking more about the revenue they can earn marketing for you, than your revenue. I'm not saying you should never work with a marketing consultant. That would be untrue because I myself help smart business owners with their marketing. What I'm saying is you're the only one who knows exactly where your business wants to go.

If you don't share that with your marketing consultant, or if the person doesn't ask you about your objectives, your goals, the revenue that you expect, or the audience you want to reach or the market you want to be in, there's something wrong. It means that the person will mostly work for himself in your marketing, rather than for you. So remember, you are your business's best marketer. Never forget that.

To have what it takes to be a good home staging business owner, not only good, but to be a great one and generate sales, you also need a USP, Unique Selling Proposition. The definition of USP is a tag line on the business card that sets you apart and that focuses on transformation. For example, Domino's Pizza delivers in 30 minutes or your pizza is free. What does it mean? It means that they give you the guarantee that you will eat within the next 30 minutes if you order pizza right now.

FedEx's USP is "When it absolutely, positively has to be there overnight". So what FedEx will do for you is to actually deliver your package or letter by tomorrow. So that's a great warranty. Actually, they focus on the transformation. They focus on the result. And that's the key to a great USP.

Too many business cards, ads, boards, have no USP to distinguish themselves from others.

Let's say for example, "In Business Since 1940." So what? What does it mean? Because you've been in business since 1940, it means that you're the best or we have to do business with you? It doesn't say anything about what you do or how different you are from all the others and why I should choose you over everybody else. So, that's USP. It means you need to be able to set yourself apart from all the other businesses in your niche.

You're basically telling people, "Well, you know what, you need to do business with me because this is what you're going to get if you do business with me. This is the transformation that you will feel or that you will have" or "This is the solution I could bring to your problems." If you do that, of course, you're going to have more chances of generating sales and have good business.

Lately, I've been to the garage with the car and I'm always reaching for business cards and looking at the marketing that businesses do. Actually the garage where I went gets most of its business by word-of-mouth. We'll talk about that later in this book but on the business card, all it said was that it has been in business since 1957. That's all it did.

It was giving me the name of the garage, the person's name, and the time of the next appointment behind the card. It was saying nothing serious. The logo was like an ordinary logo and it didn't say anything about what I would get after I left this garage. But I realized by talking to that business owner that he was very, very aware of how important it is to treat a client well. If I hadn't spoken to him, and got all this information, I wouldn't have known otherwise.

After my car was done, it was also cleaned. It's not all garages that when they repair your car, they give it back to you perfectly clean, smelling good, and fresh. I really appreciated that. Speaking to him, I'm completely sure I'll do business with him again, but then again, if I hadn't spoken to him about marketing, or about how he sees his business, or how he sees his clients, probably I would not have known.

When you have a USP, you can think about also having an "elevator pitch." An "elevator pitch" is a 30-second speech that you can give to people in order for them to be willing to ask you more. Let me give you an example. When

Excellence Home Staging was still providing Home Staging Services, here was its elevator pitch:

"Every morning, every day, every evening, the same old things: take care of the kids, go to work, help with homework, watch a little television, organize all the house chores (cleaning, laundry, ironing, shoveling, cooking...) All these things lie heavy on your shoulders... What we do is we help you to free your spirit and decrease your everyday stress. We give you the chance to live more peacefully and more healthily."

See that the elevator pitch focuses on the end result, not on the company itself. It tells the client what he should expect, how he will feel. The path taken was to go through the client's pain first, his sense of being overwhelmed. After reading this, the client wants to know more about the services we offer.

One other thing you need to have if you want to be sure that you have what it takes to be a great home staging business owner and generate sales, you need a targeted niche.

So "targeted" means a very specific niche. We have that wrong impression when we start a business that we really, really need to go broad and to be available, or to show that we could help anyone do anything, especially in home staging. For example, we want to do home staging for investors, for real estate agents, for homeowners, for condos, for high-end houses, for apartments, or for renting. If someone wants to stage an apartment for, he will more likely call the stager who specializes in rented appartments. It's no good to be too broad because, first of all, it's too much work. It will take forever for you to develop a system, create a template, so you won't have to start over again and again.

When you target a niche, if you decide to just stage condos, for example, like, 4-½ condos, you develop an expertise with that. Basically, if you position yourself as the condo home staging expert, if someone has a condo, guess who he is going to call? He is going to call the condo-expert. He is not going to call the home stager who could do the condo, the house, or this and that.

A good friend of mine shared with me that when he started his accounting business, he wanted to be available for everybody. He would do business with anybody who offered to do business with him. There was one big problem though: it was very exhausting. He felt that any time he was working with someone in another type of business, he would have to start all over again. He was trying to build a system, but it was impossible! Because anytime he had a new client, since it was in another niche, he had to start all over again.

He decided to target a niche (accounting for plumbers) and since then, his business has just boosted with sales. So the thing is, if you go too broad, there's a lack of clarity and it's very overwhelming. You need to stop thinking that there are too many home stagers in this business because there is a place for everyone.

Depending on who you want to target, your sales letters, your marketing presentations, where you're going to be at, what you write about, all that will differentiate you from your competitors, that's for sure. So take some time right now to think about which niche you want to target. And when I say the targeted niche, don't forget that you need to know where you want to target your customers. It could be Eastern USA or it could be New York. It doesn't really have to be all over the country.

# CHAPTER 2

## How Can I Make Sure That My Business Will Last?

That's a good question. One thing makes a lot of entrepreneurs fail: opportunity seeking. This is wrong. Instead, try to start being an entrepreneur. Because I assure you: this is the key to success for all business owners.

An opportunity seeker is someone who is constantly looking for "the" thing or "the most" valuable thing, or "the fastest way" to get that extra money or "the greatest system" in order to make him grow his business quicker than all the others.

That is the person who believes in the power of product launches that generate lots of sales even at the first launch without having to put that much energy into it. Product launches DO WORK. But there is a whole system behind them. It's not true that you will quickly make this huge amount of sales, just like that, without studying how it works. An opportunity seeker is someone that really has the magical thought, we could say. You know, this strong feeling that you have when you're a teenager and you think that nothing can happen to you because you are so strong?  Well, that is the true definition of an opportunity seeker.

An entrepreneur, on the other hand, is someone who is truly building a business.  Not just a little company that will survive a few months.  A long-term business that will last.  Not only does he take care of establishing his team, but he is also very good at identifying his strengths and weaknesses.  Basically he is able to delegate things that he dreads to do in order to put his energy into what he is most productive in doing.  That's an entrepreneur.

An opportunity seeker will work in sequences and not constantly, but will produce a boost of energy anytime he finds something that might put him to the next level.

On the other hand, don't get me wrong; it's not that the entrepreneur will not get excited. The entrepreneur will still get excited. He will find his core motivation by projecting himself reaching the next goal, and the next goal, and the next goal to achieve... He takes the goal he wants to achieve and rewinds it into several steps that he has to do everyday, every month, every year.

For an opportunity seeker, each opportunity is the next best thing for him.

At a seminar, I met this guy who was doing network marketing for a telecommunication business. For him, it was "the thing" to do. He was spending a lot of money and putting a lot of energy into that business and he thought that there was nothing else that could bring in more revenue in his life.

After a while, he got bored. So he decided to shift into trading. He didn't really want to invest too much, so he just learned about trading with free videos and by asking friends about it. He never seriously invested any money in his trading education. But he still wanted to earn big numbers with his transactions.

He tried a few free classes and really liked it. He finally thought, "This is it. This is my way to get more revenue." As soon as he realized that just knowing a little bit of it was not enough for him to generate that extra revenue for his family, he let that go.

Then, he started with real estate. He knew a little bit, because he had bought a condo for his family to live in. That was it. He invested into one apartment building deal, and then decided that it was not lucrative enough quickly enough for him, so he quit.

For the last five years, this man has talked about quitting his job. But guess what? He is still in the same job today. Worse, he went back to university to become a teacher and get a second job. Conflicting behavior.

One big problem that person had was that the investment into his own education was not of value to him. To him, anything had to be cheap or free. As Jim Rohn used to say: "Formal education will make you a living. Self-education will make you a fortune."

We can say that this opportunity seeker never learned how to become an entrepreneur so that's why he is turning this wheel and never ever ending it.

Let's metaphor this concept into dating. Identify whether you want a fling or you want a long-term relationship. Let's say you go out and you meet someone. Do you want that someone only for one night or do you want that someone for the rest of your life? What are you going to do?

Your energy will not be the same. When you think about a long-term relationship, what do you do? You are calmer. You see long term. You don't see getting everything right now. You are patient. You let things grow slowly. The more they grow, the more you are sure about your choice. You mature into what you're trying to build and it has so many more chances of being successful.

If you go for a fling, if you are going to someone just for one night, you never have any assurance that this person will be next to you in the morning. The person might leave. Your attitude was "only for one night oriented". You seek the opportunity but then again, did you think about long term? Even if this person that you met was the person of your life, you just let the opportunity pass by because the way you acted was not at all the way you should have acted if you wanted that person to be a long-time partner.

As Lee Milteer (intuitive business mentor) says, "If you dread to do something in your business, it's a very bad sign." It's actually directly related to a decrease of your business income. That's why it is so important to focus on what you are good at and to delegate everything else that you dread. You also need resilience to make sure that your business will last.

Resilience means the capacity to adapt or to go over something that didn't go the way you wanted it to go, to pass through a failure or to be able to stand up again, to keep moving forward, "Get hit and keep moving forward," as Rocky Balboa says to his son in *Rocky V*. Adam West (actor who played Batman) also says, "Success does not come with warning or warranty."

When success happens, there's no warning. But then again, there is no warranty that your success will continue. That's why if something happens, for example, you have a challenge or you have a failure, either a small or a big failure, that's not the end of the world because you still need to move on, to go on to keep your business rolling. Obstacles will be in the way all the time. Then, if you have a strong team, it will be easier for you to go through those hard times.

We know the story of Thomas Edison. He tried so many times before he was finally able to turn the light on. He found so many ways that the light was not working, which was really good because it helped him go closer to that time when he succeeded. Donald Trump had several bankruptcies and Jim Cramer (Trading Expert) actually once lived in his car because he didn't have any money. Those people became successful afterwards, so why not you?

The focus should be to hold on to your "why." Why are you in business?  Is it because you love to travel and your dream would be to have a home just by the beach, on a Caribbean Island? Is it because you want your kids to have the best education?  So you want to be wealthy in order to have no restrictions whatsoever into which school your kid is going to go?

Is your "why" helping a special cause because your grandmother suffered and died from cancer, and you want to help that foundation with some of the money that you earn?  So you have your "why" and you need to hold on to it. Whenever those challenges happen or those failures occur, if you can stick to your "why," it will be so much easier to get through all your problems. You need the capacity to adapt and that's going to save you. That is going to keep your business out of the water, make it successful, and go to the next level if you want.

A good example of resilience is a story about two twins. Those twins were raised with their dad. Actually, the dad was not a very good dad to his children. He beat them up. He was an alcoholic and a drug addict. One day, the twins became old enough to leave home and start their own lives. One of them got a good education. He became a lawyer. He got married to a very nice woman and had two children.

The other one was completely different. He was living on the streets, smoking, a drug addict and also an alcoholic. Maybe 20 years after they had left home, they were interviewed, because each had a different way of living. And they both answered the same thing when someone asked them: "Why did your life become that way?" The answer: "With the dad that I had what else should I have been doing?"

Moral of the story: it all depends on which side you want to be.

After a business challenge, do you want to drown or do you want to get out of the water? You are the only person who can answer this question.

Persistence, constant persistence. Do things regularly every day. Make a plan. And follow your plan. A plan is an engagement with yourself and we are so bad at that sometimes. Don't disappoint yourself.

If a friend asks you, let's say, "Would you drive me to the airport tomorrow please? I have a flight and I don't have any ride so I will count on you to do it." You're like, "Yeah sure. No problem." But then again if you have an appointment with yourself, training, because you have been wanting to train for about 2-3 months now and you are out of shape, then what do you do first thing in the morning when your alarm rings? You find an excuse in order to stay in bed longer...

It is important to have an engagement with yourself. It's also good for your self-esteem, to prove to yourself that you are someone who respects your own word. Basically, it will also help you to succeed in even more complex challenges. How bad do you want it? For sure, if you start a business in something that you don't really like or you're not passionate about, how are you going to fight for it if something happens? You need to focus on the right things. Your internal dialogue needs to be positive.

I have an example that I read in Chet Holmes' book, *The Ultimate Sales Machine*. Let's say you are in an airport or in a restaurant, in a park or any public place. There are people walking, talking, listening to music, running, doing exercises. There are so many types of people. What happens is you hear the noise but can you pay attention to all the small noises? No because you have a filter.

You have a filter that helps you go through the airport hall and get through your gate without having been so disturbed by the surrounding noise. You are able to fade it away in your brain. That's the same thing about your business. You have to be able to fade off unimportant information. But as soon as you hear a trigger that concerns you, then you absolutely need to pay attention.

Let's take the example of the airport again. If you are walking into the airport and there's a lot of noise, of course you are not going to hear anything until your spouse calls you. You are going to recognize his voice, you'll pay attention, and you'll see he *is* important information. He is the focus so you listen to him. But if a complete stranger says another name, you are not even going to pay attention, because your brain is going to take care of fading out that information.

# CHAPTER 3

## What About Sending A Postcard With My Face On It Every Time I Make A Sale With Home Staging And Hope The Owner w Will Call Me When He Is Ready To Sell?

Everybody does that. How different will you be? You could still do that, but then again, you would need pretty good copywriting. We'll talk about the components of a sales letter or a piece of copy in another chapter.

When you send your face on a nice postcard that says: "sold" and give your name and your phone number, you don't differentiate yourself from others since everybody else does it. We could just take the next stager's picture and put it on the postcard and it would exactly be the same.

People are bombarded with publications, with publicity, with advertising, with everything. So if you do not do something that draws their attention, you are seen as an uninvited mosquito instead of being an expected guest. The image I like to use when I speak about that is the vacuum cleaner consultant.

When he knocks at your door right in the middle of dinner with your family and asks you if you want to buy a new vacuum cleaner, what happens? First of all, it stresses you out.

Second, he disturbs you and third, you might not buy from him because he is doing exactly what the others are doing. He is disturbing what you were doing with your family and you don't necessarily need the vacuum cleaner at this moment in your life.

To become an expected guest, what you have to do in your communications or in your sales with your potential clients, is to create a need. So when the potential client sees your car, your ad, your publicity, your package, whatever you send to him, he sees that: "Oh wait a minute, this one is different. Oh wait a minute, I need that," or "Wait a minute. I'll call him to do business with him."

If they are not ready to do business with you, if you send your stuff enough times to that same person, because again in your research you have targeted that this person might need the type of service that you sell (here for instance home staging), I don't know why this person would not call you.

And don't forget the owners selling without real estate agents. This is also a great clientele to target.

As I said before, if you send direct mail, you must create a need and you have to show that you are the solution to their problems. In every communication that you direct at your targeted audience, you have to emphasize the downside of the alternatives. What will happen if they don't do business with you? What will happen if they don't stage and put their home on the market without you? What are the advantages of staging the property?

How much money will they lose if they don't stage their home with you? What are the statistics concerning the number of days or months that a house stays on the market if it's not staged versus if it's staged? What will happen to the buyer if he has several choices on the same street if your house is not staged? Things like that. The best way to find out what your targeted audience needs is to participate in forums, hear about their concerns.

Basically if you know about their concerns, all your copywriting will be focused on their concerns.

Now, you will ask: What about the investors? What about the fact that it would be great to do business with an investor? Sometimes, people forget about them. They buy a home, they just renovate it, and then they put it on sale. In other words, you profit from them. Sometimes they get those homes from auctions. They get the homes at a very, very low price, they invest a small amount of money, and then they sell it for big top dollar.

What's nice about it is that if you are both realtor and home stager, you have all the advantages of having the investor because first of all, you know that person is going to sell a lot of homes during the same year, so basically it's almost guaranteed revenue for you. If you do the home staging at the same time, again you could take care of the staging of each of those homes that the investor is going to sell. Usually, that person has a tendency to delegate things that he cannot do on his own.

If an investor is very satisfied with the service you provided as a realtor or home stager or both, he will probably call you again for the next house he buys. So think about that option.

# CHAPTER 4

## Are There Some Principles That I Have To Follow When I Write Copy?

First, let me define what is copywriting. Copywriting is communicating with your targeted audience in a way that they will feel understood, just as if you were talking to each person specifically, as if you understood each of their emotions. You will probably make them go from being scared to being happy, to not knowing and then being sure that your product answers their problem. This requires empathy.

## Squeeze Page

Let's take a squeeze page for example: a squeeze page is a page on your website where you have several components and then you could actually have a little box where you invite the people who land on your site to enter their name and email address in exchange for a free gift (pdf report, audio, ebook, etc).

On that page, first of all, you need a killer headline. A killer headline is a title that gives the reader no choice as to whether or not they will want to read more on your subject. Here are some examples:

- How Safe Is Your Business From Sinking?

- The Shocking Truth About List Building

- Home Seller Alert: The New Real Estate Scam To Avoid

Then you need the sub-headline, bullet points, an opt-in box, and a bribe or a free gift.

Bullet points are there for one reason. Get your reader's attention. You have all been on websites where a page is filled with information. Quickly, you want to identify whether the information is something you would be interested in or not. Well, what do you do? You scan the page. You read the titles, subtitles, bullet points, you look at the images and you read the P.S. If you are satisfied with what you see and what you read, you will pay closer attention.

An opt-in box is a quick way for you to build your list. If you are not familiar with list building, it is a way for you to market to a great number of prequalified people who have actually already raised their hand. You connect your website opt-in box with your list building account. Then, you can regularly send emails offering to send free information, and build a relationship with those people. You will eventually market to them to sell your products and services.

Why a bribe or free gift?  It will actually help you increase your email list.

If you write "Enter your name and email, and receive this free report called *How to Become a Successful Home Staging Business Owner",* you will give a great reason for someone to opt-in. Cool, it's free. If you want to read the report, you will put your email address in.

Sales Letter

When you write a sales letter, it has to control the mind of the person who reads it.  The person has to feel as if they have no power anymore.

You have control over them. Well, not necessarily in that way, but they have to feel powerless concerning their problem. They need to get emotional and excited, and then you need to write that sales purpose and create an urge to act. The person should not have a choice. They would have a choice to just click on the link or take the phone and call you. A good exercise to start with before starting your sales letter is to imagine your potential client calling you. Identify the avatar of your potential client: what he does for living, age, gender, problems, frustrations, challenges, what he secretly desires the most. For example, your targeted client could be in his mid 30's, male, not able to support his family anymore, overwhelmed by his 2 jobs and family responsibilities, feeling insecure about the economy, concerned that his home will stay on the market for too long, wanting to have some peace of mind and make the biggest amount of money as possible from selling his home so he can start over with his family. You need to have your client's avatar in mind anytime you write a sales letter.

Then, you need to express your own struggle, pains and frustration before you achieved success and fulfillment. You will appear "human" (which you are!) to your potential client and they will see in a sense how you relate to their problems. After that, show how your product or services IS the answer to all his troubles and focus on the transformation it will create for them.

Don't forget to end your letter or website page or any communication with your potential or existing client with a call to action. You absolutely need the person to do something about what he read. If he felt concerned about everything you've written, if he felt emotionally touched, scared, or powerless about his problem, for sure, he is going to click, he is going to call, he is going to do whatever it takes in order to have a solution to his problem.

On your call to action, it is very important to tell the person exactly what to do, for example:

- Pick up the phone. Dial 305-444-7777.

- Enter your name and email.

- Click here and get your 15% discount.

Be very specific.

# CHAPTER 5

## Where Should I Market My Business?

Well, we talk a lot about social media. You should be on social media. Not only should you have your website but you have to be careful about what your website looks like.

On Facebook, for a certain amount of money, you can actually enhance the visibility of your business by targeting a specific audience and showing them the ad for your business in order to maybe get them on your list or generate sales.

On Twitter, you can follow people who compete with you and your niche. It's very good for research. It's a good way to learn about what people need, what people's concerns are, and who are the dominant players in your market and what they do that works, so it could help you in your own business too.

You could also go on LinkedIn because it has several groups in your area of expertise, for instance, all the home staging groups or the real estate groups. You could get into those groups and read realtor's concerns, home staging concerns, clients' concerns. What problems other realtors have with their clients and what they needed to do to solve them.

Google +, Instagram, Pinterest, are also other platforms worth exploring to expand your audience.

Being on social media is FREE ACCESS to information, but mostly to your audience. The Hollywood stars use social media more and more to advertise new songs, new movies, new clothes. Ordinary people can be directly linked to Actors, Politicians, Entrepreneurs, and Successful People. Wow.

It's very important that all those social media accounts link to your blog because your blog is the place where you can be the authority, where you can prove that you have good content, you create value for your customer, and you know exactly what you are doing.

And offline marketing is not dead at all. People use old media. It's not true that everybody is on the Internet. Actually, there is a nice statistic that I read recently on Jeff Bullas' blog, which said that 6.6% of companies' budgets are put into social media marketing and within the next five or six years, it's going to go up to 60%. Therefore, today, it is still at 6.6%.

So yes, it's going to go up but then again, it means that there's also a certain percentage that is put into offline marketing. A good offline marketing approach is direct mail. A 3 steps sequence mail.

The first one is presenting yourself and inviting people to take action.

The second one is a reminder that you sent the first letter in.

The third one is a final notice.

In those letters, you have to write specific things in order for them to be tempted to pick up the phone, to order your program, or just to do business with you. Offer discounts; make them feel that it is urgent to act now. Have a limited time offer.

You could also target magazines that your avatar customer reads.
Market wherever your potential client is.

The Yellow Pages, yeah, why not?

In the Yellow Pages, please be different because this is the place where everybody advertises the same way! You remember when I talked a few chapters back about the garage where I went and that his advertising was no different than the others. Well, it's the same thing in the Yellow Pages. If I'm looking for a restaurant and all those restaurants are saying exactly the same thing like "great Italian food, in business since 1980, open 7 days a week…" no one of those restaurants will stand out. Similarly nobody will notice you if you use this kind of approach. You need to be different. You need to step up.

And don't forget about networking. It's all about how you look. When you do a presentation, when you do networking, or whenever you're in a crowd where you want to market your business or where you want people to remember you, dress to be noticed.

When you talk to another person, make it about him. Don't focus the conversation on you. The more you ask the person to speak about himself, the more he feels that he is accepted, he is listened to, and the more you'll also be able to answer him properly. You've got to be a very good listener when you do networking. Be out there. Get in touch with the most people that you can. In conferences, webinars, events, you need to be there.

When people see you, there's something called synergology. Synergology is your nonverbal attitude. Your synergology does not show when you're on the phone or typing an email.

When a person sees you face to face, they can put a face to your name and then they can experience your charisma. They can see your charisma in action, and appreciate all the energy that is going into your business, and that is making you the person you are.

Never ever neglect networking. You can't do business by hiding behind your desk hoping to get phone calls or generate sales. You've got to be out there. It is a great opportunity to meet business or joint venture partners.

# CHAPTER 6

## What Are The Three Biggest Marketing Mistakes Home Staging Business Owners Make?

First of all, if you don't know your client's avatar, you're in big trouble. You need to know your client's age, gender, what they do for a living, or what keeps them awake at night. If you don't do that, your offer becomes vague. Your message is not clear so nobody will feel attracted to your offer, nobody will feel deeply engaged with what you're trying to say.

It's important to target what the client wants. You are the solution to their problem. Again, don't talk about yourself.  Don't over talk about yourself.  Talk about them.  Talk about their potential transformation if they use your product.  Talk about the transformation they will feel after they receive this check of the person that put an offer on their home.  Talk about the joy that they are going to feel.

There is this story about this carpet cleaner.  He brought a list to market but the thing is, he didn't check which list he had brought.  He was doing offline marketing and sent those three sequence letters a few times.  Maybe twice during the year, he did that and didn't receive any phone calls back, didn't receive any orders.

He realized when he checked where the addresses were that he sent the marketing to, that they were in a very, very bad neighborhood with people that are very poor. They cannot even afford to have a carpet cleaner come to their home.

That's why it's very important that you know your client's avatar, and especially where they are situated. Some business owners can't market because they have no list. Their website is a brochure site. What is a brochure site? It's a site that gives you information but no call to action, no opt in box, nothing. No sign of tracking emails, no bribe or free gift. It's an empty website.

Here is an example from my personal experience. The first website I had concerning home staging, was like a brochure site, meaning that it was giving information – who I am and why I came to the home staging business, and what I can do to help people - but then again it was saying so many things about me but not enough about my avatar clients. This was before I had been to the first marketing conference I went to, when I realized that I was not generating so many sales because of my website. There was no sign of tracking emails.

But a lot of people were arriving on my site. I was number one in Google but since I had no way of tracking the emails then I could not market to all those people who were interested in home staging. So after I had been to that first conference, the GKIC Conference, I changed everything. I put in some opt-ins and then I started building my list. By doing that, it's easier to market your products, to market your services to those people because they have done the first step and they are interested in doing business with you.

One last mistake that business owners make with marketing is they focus too much on the business or on themselves instead of focusing on the client. You should always concentrate on the client in your communications. You need to generate emotions. You need to tell stories, a lot of stories because people love stories. You remember when you were a kid and your grandpa or grandma had a story to tell you, what would you do? You would just stop talking, sit down, and listen.

That's exactly what happens if you tell a story to a potential client. What the client will do, they will be very, very concentrated into hearing or reading your story, read to the end and see what happens.

Stories have this fascinating effect on us. We have to listen to them. Since a pretty young age, we are used to hear stories from our mom, dad, grand-parents, etc. When someone tells a story, we tend to listen. Period.

You also need to focus a lot on the expected transformation for the client, because if you don't do that, you lose the sale, you lose the client, and you lose the client's interest in whatever you have to sell or what you want to do for your business.

The most important thing that you have to remember in the entire book is that marketing has to focus on your client and never on you.

You need to recreate what your potential client wants or needs.  That is the only way to give a 5-star-service to all the clients that will do business with you.

Do You Want To Receive Free Bonuses?  If you do, go to www.marketingtocrushyourcompetitors.com/contact-me/ and start your message with Send Me My Bonuses!

When you do, you will receive:

- A mind map and a document on Home Staging Business Owner Success Plan

- 5 best online tools for Home Staging Business Owners

- A Getting Started With Your Home Staging Business Checklist

## About The Author

**Fabienne Raphaël** is a Bestselling Author, Serial Entrepreneur and Marketing Expert, helping Home Staging Business Owners With Their Marketing Strategy To Rise Above The Competition. She's also a Former Team Handball Olympic Athlete and won several medals and awards. She's used to compete and hates to lose! Her mission is to help as many people as possible, through her several businesses, to upgrade their quality of living and access to a higher level.

www.marketingtocrushyourcompetitors.com

ISBN-13: 978-1500260910

Marketing To Crush Your Competitors

10.80$ CAD/9.99$ USD